AF483504

PAUSE FOR 5 ON 5 TRANSFORMATIONAL MINDSET RENEWAL

MERLINE ULLOTH

The Uncommon U Press

Pause for 5 on 5™

Interrupt the overwhelm. Realign your thoughts. Return to God.

A 30-Day Devotional for the Christian Woman Who's Running on Empty

To Jesus, who led me to the pause.

To my husband and children—for loving me through the process, giving me space to heal, and cheering me on every step of the way. I love you.

And to the woman who's been running on empty—this pause is for you.

Contents

Five years ago, a car accident shifted life as I knew it—not just physically, but mentally, emotionally, and spiritually.

I had to learn to move at a pace much slower than I was used to. I had to accept that some things simply wouldn't get done. I had to grieve the woman I was before and come into alignment with the God of peace.

Still, I pushed. Still, I overextended. Still, I ran myself to exhaustion—and called it faithfulness. I called it expanding capacity. I called it resilience.

And every fall, without fail, something subtle crept in.

Not depression. Not seasonal affective disorder. Not a clinical diagnosis.

Just a heaviness—quiet, persistent, and strangely familiar.

It started as irritation. Then exhaustion. Then a foggy mental fatigue that made even simple tasks feel complicated. My body felt rundown. My thoughts scattered. My energy dimmed.

The sorrow was temporary and purposeful—but I almost missed it. Because I couldn't slow down long enough to see it. And when you don't slow down, your body eventually shuts you down.

Meanwhile, life kept accelerating.

Back-to-school schedules and endless forms. Thanksgiving cooking and hosting. Christmas shopping, wrapping, volunteering—and the emotional labor of creating memories for everyone else while feeling completely spent.

My mouth kept saying yes. My mind agreed. But my body whispered, *I can't keep doing this.*

The holidays didn't feel like holidays. They felt like survival—like putting on everyone's oxygen mask except my own.

And then I'd stumble into January, expecting the new year to work like a magic wand—as if flipping the calendar could undo months of depletion.

It didn't.

The cycle just continued—dormant through winter, masked by the bells and whistles of new year excitement.

I'd start the year ramping back up. New Year's resolutions. Bold declarations. Vision board parties. Women's conferences. Twenty-one-day community Daniel Fast. The excitement hit like a caffeine and dopamine rush—strong at first, convincing me this year would be different.

But by summer the caffeine wore off. I'd lose steam halfway through the year, mustering energy to drag myself into a second half I couldn't even see yet.

Summer sunshine promised the boost I needed. Vacation. Rest. A reset.

But by the time fall rolled around, the slow drag returned. The heaviness crept back in. And I found myself right where I started—exhausted, overwhelmed, and running on fumes again.

Somewhere between pumpkins and poinsettias, a quiet sadness slipped in.

Year after year.

THE RHYTHM THAT CHANGED EVERYTHING

It changed the day I stopped pushing.

I didn't strategize. I didn't set new goals. I didn't try to optimize my schedule.

I just stopped.

One morning, I sat with God.

Not to ask for answers. Not to fix anything. Just to sit.

And in that stillness, something surfaced—not urgency, not fear, but longing.

A quiet yearning—not to escape life, but to return. To that secret place where God meets you without noise or performance. Not a duty. A rendezvous.

"He who dwells in the secret place of the Most High..." — Psalm 91:1 (NKJV)

As I stayed there, memory followed.

I remembered my neurologist—the one who oversaw my care for nearly two years after the accident. How consistently he reminded me that healing requires rest. How gently, and firmly, he'd say the same thing:

"Five minutes will do it. Just five minutes."

He'd remind me how blessed I was and encourage me to speak that truth over myself daily.

At the time, it felt almost too simple.

That morning, as I continued sitting with God, I heard a familiar whisper:

"Continue to sit. Five minutes. Think on these things."

My attention was drawn to Paul's words in Philippians 4:8–9:

"Whatever is true, whatever is noble, whatever is right, whatever is pure, whatever is lovely, whatever is admirable—if anything is excellent or praiseworthy—think about such things... And the God of peace will be with you."

This wasn't a suggestion. It was an invitation.

And more than that—it was instruction.

So I started practicing.

Not all at once. Not perfectly.

Just five minutes.

Five minutes passed quickly—too quickly. So instead of stretching the time, I returned to the pause.

Again. And again.

I began taking five minutes every hour—only when I could. No pressure. No performance.

And then I noticed something unexpected.

My eyes naturally glanced at the clock when the minute hand landed on the five. Not every time—but often enough to matter.

So I built a rhythm around it.

Pause for 5 on 5 was born.

Not as a program. Not as a formula. But as a return.

A rendezvous woven into the ordinary hours of my day.

I became enthusiastic about meeting God throughout my day—not just once in the morning, but again and again.

At the fives.

Pausing to breathe. Pausing to think on what is true. Pausing to let my body settle. Pausing to re-anchor my mind in Him.

And something began to shift.

Peace arrived—not suddenly, but steadily.

Not because my circumstances changed, but because my presence did.

I wasn't waiting until the end of the day to exhale. I wasn't pushing through hours of tension before finally collapsing into rest.

I was returning to God while the day was still unfolding.

By design. On purpose.

This wasn't emotional hype. It wasn't denial.

It was peace—the kind that doesn't make sense on paper but holds up in real life. The kind Jesus promised. The kind the world can't manufacture.

That rhythm didn't just change my days.

It changed how I moved through life.

Less reaction. More regulation. Less striving. More listening.

And it began with something small enough to sustain.

Five minutes. At the five.

MAYBE YOU KNOW THIS FEELING

Maybe you don't have a brain injury. Maybe you've never been in an accident. Maybe your body works just fine on the outside.

But you're still exhausted.

Here's the truth no one talks about: sadness doesn't discriminate. Stress doesn't check your résumé before it shows up. Overwhelm doesn't ask permission.

It comes for all of us.

The stay-at-home mom and the executive. The minister's wife and the single woman starting over. The one recovering from trauma and the one who "has it all together."

You don't need a diagnosis to be depleted. You don't need a crisis to be running on empty. Sometimes the weight of ordinary life—carried long enough—becomes extraordinarily heavy.

Your nervous system is overloaded. Your emotions are frayed. Your mind is weary.

And somewhere deep inside, a quiet ache is saying:

"I cannot live at this pace."

"I need room to breathe."

Beloved, that ache is not weakness. It's a signal—a compassionate warning light on the dashboard of your soul.

And it led you here.

SPIRIT, SOUL, AND BODY

God didn't design you as a floating mind disconnected from your body. He created you as a whole being—spirit, soul, and body, woven together by His intentional design.

Paul prayed this over the church:

"May God himself, the God of peace, sanctify you through and through. May your whole spirit, soul and body be kept blameless." — 1 Thessalonians 5:23 (NIV)

Notice: the God of peace is the One who sanctifies your whole self.

When your spirit is neglected, your soul suffers. When your soul is weary, your body breaks down. When your body is depleted, your mind can't think clearly enough to hear God.

They are connected. Healing one heals the others. Neglecting one drains the others.

This is why *Pause for 5 on 5* doesn't just address your thoughts—it addresses your whole being. Because God's peace was never meant for just your spirit. It was designed for all of you.

HOW THIS WORKS

This devotional is built on three foundations: spiritual, physical, and practical.

Spiritually, we anchor in Philippians 4:8—training our minds to think on what is true, noble, right, pure, lovely, and admirable. Repetition of truth brings peace. Pausing creates space to hear God.

Physically, your brain needs rhythmic rest. Intentional breathing lowers cortisol and calms the nervous system. Focused attention rewires neural pathways. This isn't just spiritual discipline—it's how God designed your body to heal.

Practically, each day follows a simple rhythm:

The Reflection — Read. Absorb. Let truth speak.

The Pause — Arrive. Breathe. Settle.

Pray With Me — Talk to God. He's listening.

Declare With Me — Speak truth over your life.

Journal Prompt — Go deeper if you choose.

Each devotional takes about five minutes.

WHEN TO PAUSE

You can use this devotional any time—morning, lunch, evening, or whenever you need to reset.

But if you want to build a rhythm, here's a simple practice:

Pause once at any time that ends in :05.

For example: 7:05 AM while drinking your coffee. 12:15 PM during your lunch break. 3:25 PM when the afternoon slump hits.

Pick one time. Just one. The :05 is simply a trigger—a reminder that when the clock hits a "5," you can pause, breathe, and return to God.

Some days you'll pause once. Some days you'll return more often. There's no grade. No perfect way to do this.

The only goal is to return.

WHY NOW

You're starting this at the beginning of the year—on purpose.

Because by the time fall arrives, life will ramp up. The holidays will come. And most women will enter that season already running on empty.

But not you.

You're building the rhythm now. Learning to pause before you break. Returning to God while you still have breath—not waiting until you've run out of it.

By summer, you'll notice the shift. By fall, you'll be unshakeable.

This is the shift: proactive, not reactive.

A WORD BEFORE WE BEGIN

This devotional is a spiritual and emotional support tool designed to encourage mindfulness, nervous system regulation, and connection with God. It is not a substitute for professional medical care, mental health treatment, or therapy.

If you are experiencing persistent sadness, difficulty functioning, or thoughts of harming yourself, please seek support from a licensed counselor, therapist, or medical professional.

If you are in crisis, call **911** or the National Suicide Prevention Lifeline at **988**.

You are not alone. Help is available. Reaching out is not weakness—it is wisdom.

THE INVITATION

Beloved, you don't have to keep living at this pace.

Five minutes. That's all this takes.

Five minutes to breathe. Five minutes to think on what is true. Five minutes to return.

"Think on these things... practice these things... and the God of peace will be with you." — Philippians 4:8–9

Now turn the page. Day 1 is waiting.

DAY 1 — GIVE YOURSELF PERMISSION TO GET OFF THE SPIN CYCLE

Think on this: Whatever is TRUE

"Come to Me, all who are weary and burdened, and I will give you rest."
— Matthew 11:28 (NIV)

There comes a point when your mind feels tangled, your heart feels heavy, and your body whispers, "I can't keep doing this."

That moment is not failure—it is revelation.

It's God showing you that the pace you've been keeping is no longer sustainable for the place He is taking you.

Sometimes the most spiritual thing you can do is step out of the cycle—the cycle of overthinking, overgiving, overfunctioning, and over-riding your own needs.

You've been spinning.

Spinning in responsibility. Spinning in worry. Spinning in expectations. Spinning in trying to be everything for everyone while quietly running on empty.

You know the feeling—when you stop moving for one second and the whole room keeps going. When you lie down at night but your mind won't. When your body is begging for rest but your brain is already rehearsing tomorrow.

That's not strength. That's a spin cycle. And the only thing it's doing is making you dizzy.

Today, heaven gives you permission: Get off.

You were not created to live dizzy. You don't have to keep moving just because you always have. You don't have to hold everything together at the cost of falling apart inside.

The world won't crumble because you took your hands off what God never asked you to keep in motion.

Stopping is not quitting—it's choosing survival over self-sacrifice. It's refusing to punish your humanity for having limits.

Jesus doesn't invite the strong to prove themselves. He invites the weary to come, to stop, and to receive.

So come.

You do not have to earn the right to slow down. You only have to give yourself permission.

Today, let your soul exhale. Step out of the swirl. Let the cycle slow... and then let it stop.

You're safe. You're held. You're allowed.

THE PAUSE · 1 MINUTE

Take a breath. A slow one. Let your shoulders drop. Let your jaw unclench.

Before you read another word, acknowledge this: you're tired. Not just physically—but mentally, emotionally, spiritually.

Whisper gently: "Lord, I'm here. And I need to stop spinning."

PRAY WITH ME

Lord, I've been spinning for so long I forgot I could stop.

Today, I step off the cycle. I release the pressure to keep everything in motion. I surrender the pace that was breaking me.

Teach me to rest without guilt, to pause without panic, and to trust that You are holding what I release.

I come to You weary—and I receive Your rest.

In Jesus' name, Amen.

DECLARE WITH ME

I have permission to stop. I release what I was never meant to carry. I do not have to earn the right to rest. Stopping is not quitting—it is surviving. I am safe. I am held. I am allowed. **I am a woman who rests as an act of faith.** I step off the spin cycle today.

JOURNAL PROMPT *(optional)*

What have I been spinning in? What would it look like to step off the cycle and let God hold what I've been carrying?

DAY 2 — GOD IS NOT DISAPPOINTED IN YOU

Think on this: Whatever is TRUE

"The Lord your God is with you, the Mighty Warrior who saves. He will take great delight in you; in his love he will no longer rebuke you, but will rejoice over you with singing." — Zephaniah 3:17 (NIV)

You flinch when you pray. Not physically—but something in you braces for disappointment. You come to God already apologizing. Already explaining. Already shrinking, as if He's standing there with His arms crossed, waiting for you to get it together.

Somewhere along the way, you started believing He's frustrated with you. That He's keeping score. That He tolerates you but doesn't actually enjoy you.

That's the lie you've been carrying. And it's heavier than you realize.

But that's not the God of Scripture.

Zephaniah 3:17 tells us He is with you. He saves you. He takes great delight in you. He quiets you with His love. He rejoices over you with singing.

Read that again.

He's not sighing over you. He's singing over you.

Not when you get it right. Not when you finally measure up. Right now—in the middle of your mess, your doubt, your exhaustion—He is delighting in you.

You've been performing for approval that was already given before you did a single thing. You've been flinching at a rejection that doesn't exist in heaven.

God is not standing at a distance. He is near—closer than your next breath—and His posture toward you is not disappointment. It's relentless, pursuing, delighting love.

Yes, He corrects. Yes, He refines. But the way a Father steadies a daughter learning to walk—not the way a boss marks up your failures.

Today, release the lie.

Let go of the image of a disappointed God. That version of Him doesn't exist.

The One who formed you, who knows every failure and every fear, who sees the struggle behind your smile—He delights in you.

You are not a project to be fixed. You are a daughter to be loved.

PAUSE FOR 1 MINUTE

Place your hand over your heart.

Feel it beating—proof that you are alive and loved.

Inhale: "I am not a disappointment."

Exhale: "I am a delight to my Father."

Inhale: "I am enough."

Exhale: "I am accepted."

You don't have to earn approval.

You already have it.

PRAY WITH ME

Lord, I've been flinching. Bracing for Your disappointment. Apologizing before I even speak.

But that's not who You are.

You're not sighing over me—You're singing. You're not keeping score—You're keeping me close.

Today, I release the lie that I am too much of a mess for Your delight. I stop performing. I stop shrinking. I receive the truth that You take great delight in me—not because I've earned it, but because I'm Yours.

I am loved. I am wanted. I am Yours.

In Jesus' name, Amen.

DECLARE WITH ME

God is not disappointed in me. He is not sighing—He is singing. I release the lie of rejection. His posture toward me is delight, not disappointment. I am not a project to be fixed. I am a daughter to be loved.

JOURNAL PROMPT *(optional)*

When did I start flinching around God? What would change if I truly believed He delights in me—not someday, but right now?

DAY 3 — LAY DOWN THE LIES YOU CARRY

Think on this: Whatever is TRUE

"The weapons we fight with are not the weapons of the world. On the contrary, they have divine power to demolish strongholds. We demolish arguments and every pretension that sets itself up against the knowledge of God, and we take captive every thought to make it obedient to Christ."
— 2 Corinthians 10:4-5 (NIV)

There's a voice in your head that sounds like you—but it isn't. It knows your weak spots. It speaks in your tone. It's been talking so long you forgot to question it.

But here's what you need to know: not every thought in your head belongs to you.

Some of those beliefs didn't start as beliefs. They started as survival. Ways to make sense of pressure, neglect, comparison, or chaos. They were protective stories—until they became prisons.

What once kept you safe can slowly keep you small.

They sound like:

"If I rest, I'm lazy."

"If I don't show up, everything falls apart."

"I have to earn love by being useful."

"I'm too much."

"I'm not enough."

"God helps others—I'm not that blessed."

These are not truths. They are lies dressed in your voice. And they were never yours to carry.

Jesus said the truth will set you free. But first, you have to identify the lies.

You can't lay down what you haven't named.

So today, we pause—not to pile on more weight, but to set something down.

What lie have you been agreeing with? What narrative has been playing on repeat? What false belief has been shaping how you see yourself, God, or your future?

Bring it into the light. Say it out loud if you need to.

Then drag it to the cross. Replace it with the truth of God's Word.

The truth says God is for you. The truth says you are more than a conqueror. The truth says your weariness is not weakness—and your tired season is not your identity.

Whatever lie has been speaking over you—it loses its power the moment you stop agreeing with it.

One day you'll notice something has shifted. The voice that used to stop you won't sound like you anymore.

It will sound old. Tired. Out of place.

And the lies? They'll pass through like weather—noticed, not obeyed.

PAUSE FOR 1 MINUTE

Close your eyes. Let the noise settle.

Truth is louder than lies.

Inhale: "I lay down the lies."

Exhale: "I pick up the truth."

Inhale: "God's Word defines me."

Exhale: "Not my feelings."

The truth is setting you free.

Let it.

PRAY WITH ME

Lord, I've been carrying lies that sound like my own voice—but they're not.

Thoughts that didn't come from You. Beliefs that contradicted Your Word. Narratives that kept me small, stuck, and silent.

Today, I name them. Today, I lay them down.

Expose every lie that has made itself at home in my mind. Replace it with Your truth. Speak louder than the accuser.

I choose truth. I choose freedom. I choose to believe what You say about me.

In Jesus' name, Amen.

DECLARE WITH ME

I lay down the lies I've been carrying. Not every thought in my head belongs to me. I am not defined by what the enemy whispered. I am defined by what my Father declared. The truth sets me free. The lies lose power when I stop agreeing.

JOURNAL PROMPT *(optional)*

What lie have I been believing about myself, God, or my future? What truth from Scripture can I replace it with today?

DAY 4 — HE SEES YOU, EVEN HERE

Think on this: Whatever is LOVELY

"She gave this name to the Lord who spoke to her: 'You are the God who sees me,' for she said, 'I have now seen the One who sees me.'" — Genesis 16:13 (NIV)

You're pouring out—but no one seems to notice. Not that you're searching for applause. Just a little gratitude. A little *I see you—thank you.* A little acknowledgment that you're holding things together while quietly falling apart.

But the thank-yous don't come. No one asks how you're really doing. And sometimes you wonder: *Does anyone even know I'm here?*

Hagar understood.

Alone in the wilderness. Pregnant. Rejected. Running from pain with no clear destination. She had every reason to believe she was forgotten—discarded by the very people who should have protected her.

Picture her: dust on her feet, sun on her back, fear in her chest. No plan. No provision. No one looking for her.

But then God met her.

Not with correction. Not with a lecture. Not with a to-do list.

He met her with presence. With acknowledgment. With the gift of being truly seen.

And her response? She gave Him a name no one else had spoken: *El Roi*—"The God who sees me."

Whatever wilderness you're walking through today—you are not invisible to God.

He sees you in your exhaustion. He sees you in your disappointment. He sees you when you smile in public but cry in private. He sees the version of you that no one else gets access to—and He doesn't look away.

Your nakedness does not scare Him. He already knows the deal.

You don't have to perform for His attention. You don't have to prove your worth. You don't have to shout to be heard.

He is already watching. Already listening. Already near.

And He doesn't just see your struggle—He sees your strength. He sees your faith, even when it feels fragile. He sees your fight, even when you feel like giving up.

Today, let this be enough: You are seen. Fully. Tenderly. Completely.

El Roi has His eyes on you.

PAUSE FOR 1 MINUTE

Lift your eyes, even if just for a moment.

You are seen.

Inhale: "I am seen."

Exhale: "I am known."

Inhale: "I am loved."

Exhale: "I am not invisible."

El Roi—the God who sees—

is watching over you right now.

PRAY WITH ME

Lord, I confess there are days I feel invisible—overlooked by people and forgotten by the world.

But You are El Roi, the God who sees.

You saw Hagar in her wilderness. You see me in mine. Thank You for not looking away. Thank You for noticing what no one else does.

Help me stop performing for attention and start resting in the truth that I am already seen—fully, tenderly, and completely—by You.

In Jesus' name, Amen.

DECLARE WITH ME

I am seen by the God who never looks away. My invisible seasons are not invisible to Him. I do not have to shout to be heard. El Roi has His eyes on me. I am fully known and deeply loved.

JOURNAL PROMPT *(optional)*

Where have I felt invisible lately—and what does it mean to me that God sees me even there?

DAY 5 — RETURN TO THE VOICE OF THE SHEPHERD

Think on this: Whatever is NOBLE

"My sheep listen to my voice; I know them, and they follow me."
— John 10:27 (NIV)

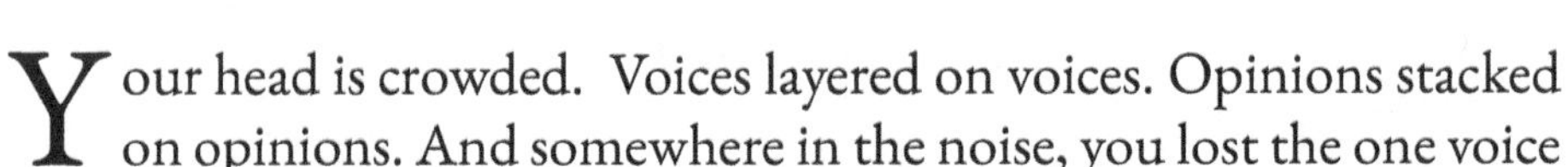

Your head is crowded. Voices layered on voices. Opinions stacked on opinions. And somewhere in the noise, you lost the one voice that actually matters.

You know the feeling—lying awake at 2 a.m. while your mind replays conversations that haven't happened. Scrolling while a dozen strangers tell you who to be, what to want, how to measure your worth. Carrying the weight of expectations you never agreed to.

The voice of comparison. The voice of fear. The voice of past failures. The voice of other people's opinions.

It's not just noise. It's chaos masked as guidance. And it's exhausting.

But Jesus said something that cuts through it all: *"My sheep listen to my voice."*

Not voices. Voice. Singular.

There is one voice that leads to life. One voice that brings peace. One voice that knows the path and won't lead you astray.

The Shepherd's voice.

He knows your name. He knows your story. He knows your capacity and your calling. And here's what the chaos won't tell you—He's not shouting over the noise. He never has been.

He's whispering in the stillness. Waiting for you to get quiet enough to hear.

"This is the way. Walk in it."

His voice doesn't condemn—it guides. His voice doesn't pressure—it invites. His voice doesn't confuse—it clarifies.

When life gets loud, your soul needs recalibration. Not more input. Not another opinion. Just a return to the familiar, trustworthy voice of the One who laid down His life for you.

Today, let the other voices fade.

Stop straining to hear everyone else. Stop crowdsourcing your peace. Come back to the Shepherd.

He hasn't stopped speaking. You just need to stop and listen.

Return to His voice. It's the only one leading you home.

PAUSE FOR 1 MINUTE

Cup your hands around your ears.

Block the noise. Listen for the Shepherd.

Inhale: "I know His voice."

Exhale: "I follow Him."

Inhale: "I tune out the noise."

Exhale: "I tune into truth."

His voice leads to peace.

Follow it.

PRAY WITH ME

Lord, my head is crowded. I've been listening to too many voices—and it has left me confused, exhausted, and lost.

Today, I return to You.

Quiet the noise around me and within me. Help me recognize Your voice above all others. Tune my heart to hear You clearly.

I don't need a thousand opinions. I need Your direction.

Speak, Shepherd. Your sheep is listening.

In Jesus' name, Amen.

DECLARE WITH ME

My head is no longer crowded with chaos. I am a sheep who knows the Shepherd's voice. I tune out the noise and tune in to Him. His voice doesn't condemn—it guides. I follow where He leads. I return to the only voice that leads to life.

JOURNAL PROMPT *(optional)*

What voice have I been listening to that isn't the Shepherd's? What would it look like to return to His voice today?

DAY 6 — DON'T RUN, COME

Think on this: Whatever is RIGHT

"Come to me, all you who are weary and burdened, and I will give you rest." — Matthew 11:28 (NIV)

You've been running again. Not literally—but your soul has been sprinting. Away from the ache. Away from the stillness. Away from the thing you don't want to feel. You scroll. You fix other people's problems. You fill every silence with sound. You stay busy enough that you never have to sit with what's underneath.

When emotions feel inconvenient, you push them down. When your needs feel like too much, you shrink them. When falling apart doesn't feel like an option, you hold it together on the outside while quietly unraveling within.

And the running works—until it doesn't.

Because running never leads to rest. It only leads to exhaustion dressed up as productivity.

Here's what no one tells you: you've been saying yes to every invitation except the one that matters. Yes to what drains you. Yes to what demands from you. Yes to everyone else's urgency.

And no to the One who simply says, "Come."

Not "Come when you're cleaned up." Not "Come when you've got it together."

Just: *Come.*

Come tired. Come messy. Come undone.

But we don't come to Him on purpose, do we? We collapse into Him by default—after we've tried everything else, exhausted every option, and hit the wall we were running toward all along.

And still—He holds us. He covers us. He whispers, "I've been waiting. I'm not disappointed that you need Me."

Remember Martha? Spinning in the kitchen. Doing all the right things for all the wrong reasons. And Mary? Sitting at His feet while the to-do list screamed.

Jesus protected Mary's choice: *"She has chosen what is better, and it will not be taken from her."*

Sometimes the most spiritual thing you can do is stop doing and start sitting.

Today, stop running. Come on purpose—not by default.

He's not asking you to earn your seat. He's already saved it.

PAUSE FOR 1 MINUTE

Unclench your fists.

Stop running. Simply come.

Inhale: "I stop running."

Exhale: "I come to Jesus."

Inhale: "He is not angry."

Exhale: "He is waiting."

You don't have to have it together.

Just come.

PRAY WITH ME

Lord, I've been running. Running from rest. Running from stillness. Running from the ache I didn't want to feel.

I've said yes to everyone else's invitation and ignored Yours. Forgive me.

Today, I stop. I come.

Not cleaned up. Not put together. Just me—weary, burdened, undone.

I'm done collapsing into You by default. I come on purpose.

Meet me here. Give me rest.

In Jesus' name, Amen.

DECLARE WITH ME

I stop running. I come to God on purpose—not by default. His invitation is for the weary, and that includes me. I don't have to earn my seat—He already saved it. I choose the better thing. I sit at His feet and receive.

JOURNAL PROMPT *(optional)*

What have I been running from? What would it look like to come to Jesus first—on purpose—instead of collapsing into Him by default?

DAY 7 — GUARD THE GATES OF YOUR MIND

Think on this: Whatever is PURE

"Above all else, guard your heart, for everything you do flows from it."
— Proverbs 4:23 (NIV)

Your mind is not an open field. It's a guarded city. And like any city, it has gates—entry points that determine what gets in and what stays out. But here's the problem: you've been leaving the gates wide open.

You know the feeling. You pick up your phone for "just a minute" and thirty minutes later your peace is gone. You scroll past something that plants a seed of comparison, and by noon it's grown into a forest of not-enough. You replay a conversation—an offense you should have released—and now it's living rent-free in your head.

That's what happens when the gates are unguarded. Anything can walk in. Fear. Comparison. Anxiety. Offense. Lies seeping in as logic.

And once they're in, they don't just visit. They settle. They spread. They start rearranging the furniture.

Proverbs 4:23 says to guard your heart *above all else*—because every-thing you do flows from it. Your thoughts shape your emotions. Your emotions shape your actions. Your actions shape your life.

The invasion doesn't start with a loud crash. It starts with an unguarded scroll. An entertained thought. A conversation you should have walked away from.

But here's the truth that changes everything: you have the authority to close those gates.

You are the gatekeeper.

You get to decide what enters and what doesn't. You get to filter what you see, hear, and entertain through the truth of God's Word.

This doesn't mean you hide from reality. It means you filter reality through truth.

You can be informed without being consumed. You can be aware without being anxious. You can engage without being overtaken.

Today, take inventory. What have you been letting in that's been stealing your peace? What gate has been left wide open?

Close it. Guard it. Protect what God has given you.

What you let in will determine what comes out.

PAUSE FOR 1 MINUTE

Place your hands on your temples.

You are the gatekeeper of your mind.

Inhale: "I guard my heart."

Exhale: "I guard my mind."

Inhale: "I choose what enters."

Exhale: "I reject what harms."

Not everything deserves access.

Guard the gate.

PRAY WITH ME

Lord, I confess I've left gates wide open that should have been guarded. I've let fear walk in through my phone. I've let comparison settle in through a scroll. I've entertained offense until it made itself at home.

Today, I take back authority over my mind.

Help me guard what I see, hear, and entertain. Give me wisdom to know what to engage and what to release. Strengthen me to protect the peace You've given me.

I close the gates. I set my mind on things above. I choose truth.

In Jesus' name, Amen.

DECLARE WITH ME

I am the gatekeeper of my mind. I guard what I let in. I protect my peace. The enemy cannot settle where he is not welcomed. I set my mind on things above. What enters my gates will align with God's truth.

JOURNAL PROMPT *(optional)*

What gate have I left unguarded? What has been walking into my mind that I need to stop allowing access?

DAY 8 — REST IN PEACE

Think on this: Whatever is NOBLE

"He makes me lie down in green pastures, he leads me beside quiet waters, he refreshes my soul. — Psalm 23:2-3 (NIV)

The enemy has a strategy for your life, and it's not complicated: keep her exhausted. How easy is it to come to agreement without even recognizing it? Exhausted women don't pray with power. They don't dream with clarity. They don't fight with focus. They simply survive—one tired day at a time.

But God has a counter-strategy: rest.

Not rest as a luxury. Not rest as a reward. Rest as a weapon.

When you rest, you interrupt the enemy's plan to wear you down. When you pause, you reclaim ground he tried to steal through busyness. When you stop—even for five minutes—you declare that your worth is not tied to your productivity.

The world says, "Do more to be more."

God says, "Be still and know that I am God."

Notice the order in Psalm 23. The Shepherd doesn't lead you into the valley and then offer rest. He makes you lie down first. He leads you to still waters first. He restores your soul *before* He guides you along the right path. *Before* the shadow of death. *Before* the enemy's table.

This is strategy.

God doesn't prepare you for battle by running you ragged. He prepares you by filling you up. The still waters come before the dark valley because you cannot walk through what you were never strengthened for.

You work from rest—not toward it. This is the rhythm of heaven: Sabbath came before labor. Adam's first full day was a day of rest. He didn't earn it. He received it. He worked from a place of already being filled—not from striving to prove his worth.

So today, reframe rest.

It is not selfish. It is sacred. It is not optional. It is essential. It is not passive. It is one of the most powerful forms of spiritual warfare you can practice.

When you rest, you are not giving up. You are gaining ground.

PAUSE FOR 1 MINUTE

Sit back. Let your shoulders drop.

Rest is warfare.

Inhale: "Rest is not weakness."

Exhale: "Rest is warfare."

Inhale: "I fight by resting."

Exhale: "I win by trusting."

The enemy wants you exhausted.

Rest is your resistance.

PRAY WITH ME

Lord, forgive me for treating rest like a reward instead of a rhythm. Forgive me for believing the lie that my value comes from my output. Today, I take up rest as a weapon. I refuse to let exhaustion be my identity. I will pause—not because I've earned it, but because You command it. My rest is an act of worship. My stillness is an act of trust. Teach me to work from rest, not toward it. In Jesus' name, Amen.

DECLARE WITH ME

Rest is not weakness—it is warfare. I am not lazy—I am strategic. My pause interrupts the enemy's plan for my exhaustion. I work from rest—not toward it. **I rest as an act of faith—this is who I am.** I am gaining ground, not giving up.

JOURNAL PROMPT (optional)

What valley am I facing—or about to face—that I've been trying to enter without first being restored? What would it look like to let God lead me to still waters first?

DAY 9 — YOU HAVE THE RIGHT TO REMAIN SILENT

Think on this: Whatever is NOBLE

"He was oppressed and afflicted, yet he did not open his mouth."
— Isaiah 53:7 (NIV)

Not every accusation requires a defense. Not every conflict requires your voice. Not every offense requires a response. You have the right to remain silent. But you haven't been using it.

You know the feeling—lying awake replaying the conversation, rehearsing what you should have said, crafting the perfect response to someone who will never hear it. You've spent hours composing texts you'll never send, winning arguments in your head while losing sleep in your bed.

And even when you do respond? It rarely brings the peace you hoped for. You walk away more drained, not less. More tangled, not free.

Here's what no one tells you: the pressure to respond is costing you more than the silence ever would.

We live in a world that rewards quick comebacks, sharp responses, and having the last word. But wisdom often looks like a closed mouth.

Proverbs 17:28 says even fools are thought wise when they keep silent. There is power in restraint. There is strength in holding your tongue.

Jesus modeled this.

When falsely accused before Pilate, He didn't argue. He didn't explain. He didn't defend Himself. The King of the universe stood silent before a Roman governor—not because He had nothing to say, but because some battles aren't won with words.

His silence wasn't weakness. It was authority.

Sometimes the most powerful thing you can do is say nothing.

Not because you don't have words—but because some situations don't deserve them.

Not because you're afraid—but because you're wise enough to know that not every battle is yours to fight.

Silence protects your peace. Silence preserves your energy. Silence lets God be your defender—and He's better at it than you.

You don't have to explain yourself to everyone. You don't have to win every argument. You don't have to respond to every jab, accusation, or misunderstanding.

Some things are better left to God. Some words are better left unsaid.

Today, release the pressure to speak. Give yourself permission to be quiet. Trust that your silence is not surrender—it's strategy.

You have the right to remain silent.

Use it.

PAUSE FOR 1 MINUTE

Press your lips together gently.

Silence is permission.

Inhale: "I have the right to remain silent."

Exhale: "I don't owe everyone an explanation."

Inhale: "My peace is protected."

Exhale: "My silence is strength."

Not every accusation deserves a defense.

Be still.

PRAY WITH ME

Lord, I have exhausted myself trying to respond to everything. I've replayed conversations at 2 a.m. I've crafted responses to people who weren't even listening. I've fought battles in my head that stole peace from my heart.

Today, I lay that down.

I don't have to defend myself to everyone. I don't have to win every argument. I don't have to have the last word.

You are my defender. You are my vindicator. I release it to You.

In Jesus' name, Amen.

DECLARE WITH ME

I have the right to remain silent—and I will use it. Not every conflict requires my response. My silence is not weakness—it is wisdom. God is my defender. I don't have to prove myself. I choose peace over proving a point. Some battles are better left unfought.

JOURNAL PROMPT *(optional)*

What situation have I been mentally rehearsing a response to? What would it cost me to let it go—and what might I gain?

DAY 10-STOP REHEARSING WORST CASE SCENARIO

Think on this: Whatever is TRUE

"Therefore do not worry about tomorrow, for tomorrow will worry about itself. Each day has enough trouble of its own."
— Matthew 6:34 (NIV)

You've been living in a future that doesn't exist yet. You've rehearsed the hard conversation a hundred times. You've imagined the rejection, the failure, the loss. You've braced yourself for the worst-case scenario—and in doing so, you've already lived through trauma that never happened.

This is what anxiety does. It borrows trouble from tomorrow and makes you pay the emotional bill today.

But Jesus said, "Do not worry about tomorrow." Not because tomorrow isn't real—but because you're not there yet. And when you get there, grace will meet you.

Grace isn't early. It shows up right on time.

So why are you mentally rehearsing moments that grace hasn't been released for? Why are you emotionally responding to events that haven't occurred?

Your nervous system doesn't know the difference between a real threat and an imagined one. Every time you rehearse the worst-case scenario, your body responds as if it's already happening—cortisol rises, muscles tense, peace disappears.

Today, stop rehearsing. Stop preparing for catastrophe. Stop spending your emotional resources on fictional futures.

Stay here. Stay now. Today has enough of its own needs—and today has enough grace to meet them.

PAUSE FOR 1 MINUTE

Place your feet flat on the floor.

You are here. Not tomorrow. Here.

Inhale: "Today has enough."

Exhale: "I stay present."

Inhale: "Tomorrow has its own grace."

Exhale: "I don't need it yet."

Stop rehearsing tomorrow's trouble.

Be here now.

PRAY WITH ME

Lord, I've been living in a future that hasn't happened yet. I've exhausted myself rehearsing worst-case scenarios, borrowing trouble that may never come.

Today, I release the future. I stop living in imagined outcomes. I trust You with what I cannot control.

Bring my mind back to today—where Your grace is enough.

In Jesus' name, Amen.

DECLARE WITH ME

I stop rehearsing worst-case scenarios. Tomorrow is not my responsibility today. Grace shows up when I get there. I release the future I cannot control. Today is where I live—and today is enough.

JOURNAL PROMPT *(optional)*

What future scenario have I been rehearsing that hasn't even happened? What would it feel like to trust God with it instead?

DAY 11-YOU HAVE EVERYTHING YOU NEED IN JESUS

Think on this: Whatever is
EXCELLENT

"The Lord is my shepherd, I lack nothing." — Psalm 23:1 (NIV)

There's always something more. More to achieve. More to fix. More to prove. More to become before you finally feel like enough. You chase the next milestone thinking it will quiet the ache. The promotion. The relationship. The recognition. The

breakthrough. But every time you arrive, the finish line moves. The hunger stays.

You know the feeling—that low hum of insufficiency that follows you into every room. The quiet voice that whispers, "You're still not there yet. You're still missing something."

But what if the ache was never meant to be filled by arriving? What if it was meant to be filled by a Person?

The Psalmist declared something audacious:

"The Lord is my shepherd; I shall not want."

Not "I shall not want for much." Not "I shall not want if I try harder." Not "I shall not want once I finally get my life together."

I. Shall. Not. Want.

This is a declaration of divine sufficiency. It doesn't mean life will be easy or that every desire will be fulfilled the way you imagined. It means that in Christ, you are not lacking.

He is your portion. And when He is your portion, you have everything you need.

He is your provision—so you can stop hustling for security. He is your protection—so you can stop bracing for disaster. He is your peace—so you can stop earning your rest.

The world will always move the finish line. It will always tell you that you need more to be more.

But heaven has a different word: You are complete in Christ. Not when you arrive. Not when you achieve. Now.

Fullness isn't a feeling; it's a Person.

And He already lives inside you.

Today, stop striving to become enough. Start resting in the One who already is.

You have everything you need—because you have Him.

PAUSE FOR 1 MINUTE

Open your hands. Receive.

You already have everything you need.

Inhale: "The Lord is my shepherd."

Exhale: "I shall not want."

Inhale: "I am not lacking."

Exhale: "I am not behind."

In Jesus, you are complete.

Nothing missing. Nothing broken.

PRAY WITH ME

Lord, I've been chasing. Chasing approval, chasing security, chasing the next thing I thought would finally make me feel whole.

But the finish line kept moving. And the ache never left.

Today, I stop.

I stop striving to become enough. I receive the truth that in You, I already am. You are my shepherd—I shall not want. You are my portion—I lack nothing.

Fill the ache that achievements never could. Be my enough.

In Jesus' name, Amen.

DECLARE WITH ME

The Lord is my shepherd—I shall not want. I am not lacking. I am not behind. I stop chasing what was never meant to fill me. I have everything I need in Jesus. Fullness is not a feeling—it is a Person. And He already lives in me.

JOURNAL PROMPT *(optional)*

What have I been chasing to fill an ache that only Jesus can satisfy? What would change if I truly believed I already have everything I need in Him?

DAY 12 — LET THEM MISUNDERSTAND YOU

Think on this: Whatever is PURE

"Am I now trying to win the approval of human beings, or of God? Or am I trying to please people? If I were still trying to please people, I would not be a servant of Christ." — Galatians 1:10 (NIV)

There's a special kind of exhaustion that comes from over-explaining yourself. From defending every decision. Justifying every boundary. Softening every no. Editing your truth so others will finally understand you.

You know the feeling—the tightness in your chest when you hit send on the paragraph-long text that should have been two sentences. The mental rehearsal of conversations where you explain, defend, clarify—again. The weight of carrying everyone's perception like it's your responsibility to manage.

It's exhausting. And it's not yours to carry.

Here's the freedom no one told you about: You don't owe everyone an explanation.

Not every raised eyebrow deserves a response. Not every whispered assumption needs to be corrected. Not every misunderstanding is yours to fix.

Jesus Himself was constantly misunderstood—by the religious elite, by the crowds, even by His own family. They called Him demon-possessed. They questioned His authority. They doubted His mission.

And yet, He didn't chase after every critic. He didn't rewrite His purpose to satisfy the confused. He kept walking toward the cross while people drew the wrong conclusions.

There is power in holy silence. There is freedom in letting people wonder.

When you stop exhausting yourself trying to manage everyone's perception, you have more energy for what actually matters—your peace, your purpose, and your presence with God.

You give account to God—not to everyone with an opinion.

Let them misunderstand you. Let them draw the wrong conclusions. Let them talk.

Your obedience doesn't require their approval. Your peace doesn't depend on their understanding. Your worth isn't determined by their perception.

And sometimes, walking in truth means staying quiet when every part of you wants to explain.

Let them wonder.

God knows.

PAUSE FOR 1 MINUTE

Release your jaw. Soften your face.

You don't have to explain yourself.

Inhale: "I let go of the need to be understood."

Exhale: "God understands me fully."

Inhale: "I release their opinions."

Exhale: "I rest in His approval."

Let them misunderstand.

God knows.

PRAY WITH ME

Lord, I am tired of explaining myself. Tired of editing my truth so others will accept me. Tired of carrying the burden of being understood by people who aren't even trying to understand.

Today, I lay that weight down.

I release the need for approval from people and receive the approval I already have from You. Help me to walk in obedience even when it's misunderstood. Help me to speak when You say speak and stay silent when You say stay silent.

I give account to You—and You alone.

In Jesus' name, Amen.

DECLARE WITH ME

I do not owe everyone an explanation. Not every misunderstanding is mine to fix. I give account to God—not to everyone's opinion. My obedience does not require their approval. My peace does not depend on their understanding. **I rest in God's understanding. He knows me fully.** Let them wonder. God knows.

JOURNAL PROMPT *(optional)*

Who have I been exhausting myself trying to make understand me—and what would it feel like to let them misunderstand and still walk in peace?

DAY 13 — URGENT SHOUTS, IMPORTANT SUSTAINS

Think on this: Whatever is RIGHT

"There is a time for everything... a time to be silent and a time to speak." — Ecclesiastes 3:1, 7 (NIV)

The pressure to respond immediately is a lie disguised as urgency. That text demanding an answer. That email marked "urgent." That confrontation waiting for your reaction. That question you're not ready to answer. That family member expecting a decision before you've had time to breathe.

The world says: Respond now. Don't leave them waiting. Handle it. Fix it. Address it.

But wisdom says: Pause.

Here's what most exhausted women have never been taught: not everything that feels urgent actually is.

Urgent things shout. They send notifications. They guilt you into responding. They create the illusion of importance by being loud.

But important things? They don't scream. Rest doesn't demand your attention. Prayer doesn't send reminders. Healing doesn't guilt-trip you into showing up. Your soul doesn't ping your phone.

And because the important things are quiet, they get neglected—until they become emergencies.

You skip rest until your body breaks down. You avoid hard conversations until they explode. You neglect your soul until anxiety takes over.

Then you wonder why everything feels like a crisis.

Jesus saw this play out in real time.

Martha was busy—serving, preparing, handling everything that felt urgent. Mary sat at His feet, choosing presence over productivity. When Martha complained, Jesus didn't validate her urgency.

He said: *"Martha, Martha, you are worried and upset about many things, but few things are needed—or indeed only one. Mary has chosen what is better."*

Martha was doing good things. Urgent things. Things that needed to be done.

But Mary chose the important thing. And Jesus protected her choice.

Sometimes the most spiritual thing you can do is stop doing and start sitting.

So when that text comes in and your chest tightens—pause. Ask yourself: Is this truly urgent? Or does it just feel that way?

You are allowed to say:

"Let me think about that." "I need time to process." "I'll get back to you." "Not right now."

These are not avoidance. They are wisdom. They are boundaries dressed in grace.

Here's a rule to carry with you:

Urgent shouts. Important sustains. Choose what sustains first.

Today, release the pressure of immediacy. You don't have to respond right now. Your peace is worth more than their timeline.

Let them wait. Your soul is more important than their schedule.

PAUSE FOR 1 MINUTE

Pause the mental to-do list.

Urgent is not always important.

Inhale: "Urgent shouts."

Exhale: "Important sustains."

Inhale: "I choose what sustains."

Exhale: "I release what distracts."

Not everything loud deserves your attention.

Choose wisely.

PRAY WITH ME

Lord, I have been living at the mercy of what shouts instead of what sustains. I've treated every notification like an emergency. I've been Martha when You were inviting me to be Mary.

Forgive me for letting urgency dictate my life.

Teach me to discern the difference between what feels pressing and what is truly important. Help me protect what sustains my soul. Give me courage to say "not right now" without guilt.

I release the pressure. I embrace the pause. I choose what's important over what's loud.

In Jesus' name, Amen.

DECLARE WITH ME

I don't have to respond right now. Not everything urgent is important. Urgent shouts—but important sustains. I choose what sustains first. I am not Martha—I choose the better thing. My peace is worth more than their timeline.

JOURNAL PROMPT *(optional)*

What important thing have I been neglecting because it doesn't shout at me? Where have I been Martha when Jesus was inviting me to be Mary?

DAY 14 — GET OUT OF YOUR HEAD

Think on this: Whatever is TRUE

"You will keep in perfect peace those whose minds are steadfast, because they trust in you." — Isaiah 26:3 (NIV)

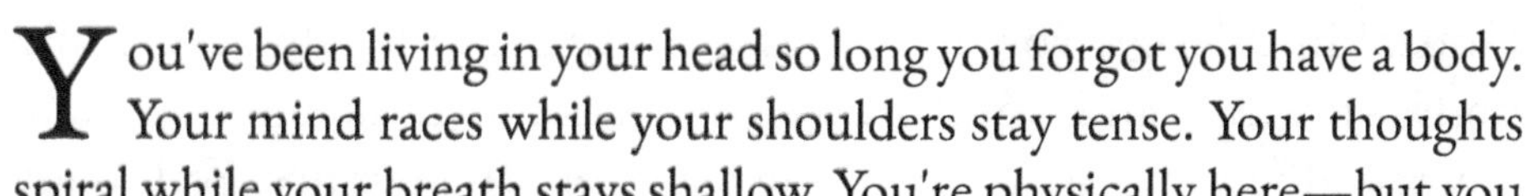

You've been living in your head so long you forgot you have a body. Your mind races while your shoulders stay tense. Your thoughts spiral while your breath stays shallow. You're physically here—but you left a long time ago.

You're in the room but not in the moment. Present in body, but unaccounted for mentally. I'm here—but I'm not really here. This is what it means to live from the neck up.

You've trained yourself to think your way through everything. Analyze. Anticipate. Strategize. Control. Your brain became the command center, and your body became background noise—something to push through, override, or ignore.

But your body hasn't been silent. It's been screaming.

This is what it looks like when your nervous system has been hijacked: The tension in your neck. The tightness in your chest. The exhaustion that sleep doesn't fix. The startle response that fires too easily. The exhaustion that sleep doesn't fix. The startle response that fires too easily.These aren't just symptoms of a busy life. They're signals that your body has been stuck in high alert—waiting for a threat that may never come.

You've been living in survival mode. And survival mode was never meant to be a permanent address.

When your body stays in fight-or-flight, it doesn't know the difference between real danger and imagined pressure. A difficult email feels like a crisis. A hard conversation feels like an attack. Silence feels unsafe. Rest feels irresponsible. Your system stays activated because somewhere along the way, it learned that letting your guard down was too risky.

So you kept thinking. Kept planning. Kept controlling. Kept living in your head because at least there you felt like you had some power.

But here's the truth: your head was never meant to be your home.

God didn't design you to live as a floating brain. He gave you a body—fearfully and wonderfully made—not as an inconvenience to your productivity but as a dwelling place for His presence. Your body is not separate from your spirituality. It's the vessel through which you experience peace, feel His nearness, and know that you are safe.

Isaiah 30:15 doesn't say, "In strategizing and striving shall be your strength."

It says: *In returning and rest you shall be saved. In quietness and trust shall be your strength.*

Returning. That's a movement—a coming back. Coming back to rest. Coming back to your body. Coming back to the present moment where God actually dwells.

Quietness. That's not just external silence. It's internal stillness. A nervous system that has permission to stand down. A mind that doesn't have to solve everything before it can be at peace.

Trust. That's the anchor. You can quiet your body and still your mind because you trust the One who holds what you cannot control.

This is the peace that calms your nervous system—not a peace you think your way into, but a peace you return to. A peace that settles into your cells and tells your body, *"You can stand down now. You are safe. The battle is not yours to fight today."*

Getting out of your head is not about thinking less. It's about living more. It's about returning to your body. Noticing your breath. Feeling your feet on the floor. Becoming aware that you are here—not in yesterday, not in tomorrow, but now.

God's name is I AM. Present tense. He is the God of right now. And He's been waiting for you to meet Him here.

You've been gone too long.

Come back to your body. Come back to this moment. Come back to the only place where peace actually lives.

Your head is not your home. But you can come home now.

PAUSE FOR 1 MINUTE

Place your hand on your chest.

Come back to your body. You're safe here.

Inhale: "My head is not my home."

Exhale: "I return to rest."

Inhale: "I am safe in my body."

Exhale: "I am present here."

Your mind may race,

but your body can be still.

PRAY WITH ME

Lord, I have been living in my head—spinning, strategizing, surviving. My body has been stuck in high alert, and I've ignored every signal to slow down. I've treated rest as weakness and stillness as wasted time.

Forgive me.

Today, I return. I come back to my body. I come back to this moment. I come back to You.

Quiet my nervous system. Settle my racing thoughts. Teach me that I don't have to figure everything out to be at peace. Help me trust You with what I cannot control.

In returning and rest, I am saved. In quietness and trust, I find my strength.

I stop surviving. I start living.

In Jesus' name, Amen.

DECLARE WITH ME

I get out of my head and come back to my body. My head is not my home. I was not designed to live in survival mode. In returning and rest, I am saved. In quietness and trust is my strength. My nervous system has permission to stand down. I am here. I am present. I am safe. Peace is not something I think my way into—it's something I return to.

JOURNAL PROMPT *(optional)*

What signals has my body been sending that I've been ignoring? What would it feel like to give my nervous system permission to stand down?

DAY 15 — YOU ARE NOT BEHIND

Think on this: Whatever is LOVELY

"At the right time, I, the Lord, will make it happen."

— Isaiah 60:22 (NLT)

I should have had the baby by now. I should be married by now. I should have the promotion by now. I should be walking in my calling by now. There's a silent pressure that builds when we compare timelines. You see where others are and where you're not. You start to believe you've missed your time—that the window closed while you were still getting ready.

But here's the truth: the only "behind" that exists is the one you invented—or the one the world handed you.

Heaven never said you were late. The timeline you created in your head—with milestones and deadlines and "by this age" markers—was never His plan. He sees what you cannot see and knows what you cannot know.

You mapped out the journey. God is writing the story. And His story doesn't follow your outline.

Your calling is not canceled because it hasn't manifested yet. Your promise is not expired because it's taking longer than you expected. God is not in a hurry—but He is always on time.

"When the time is right, I, the Lord, will make it happen." — Isaiah 60:22

He's not withholding to punish you. He's developing something you can't rush. You're not just waiting, God is actively working.

God's ways are not your ways. Beloved, be encouraged: *"He has made everything beautiful in its time."* — Ecclesiastes 3:11

And Habakkuk reminds us: *"Though it linger, wait for it; it will certainly come and will not delay."* — Habakkuk 2:3

Open your hands and give it to God. You cannot hustle your way to the promise through performance or comparison. Let patience have her perfect work in you.

Jesus—the Messiah Himself—often said, *"My time has not yet come."* If the Son of God could wait for His Father's timing, so can you.

You are not behind. You are being refined. And refining takes time.

PAUSE FOR 1 MINUTE

Release the pressure in your shoulders.

You are not behind.

Inhale: "I am not behind."

Exhale: "I am being refined."

Inhale: "God's timing is perfect."

Exhale: "I trust His pace."

You're not late.

You're on time.

PRAY WITH ME

Lord, I've been measuring myself by timelines You never set. I've called myself late, behind, forgotten.

But Your ways are not my ways. Today, I release my timeline and trust Yours. My calling is not canceled. My promise is not expired. You make everything beautiful in its time.

When the time is right, You will make it happen. I am not behind. I am exactly where You have me.

In Jesus' name, Amen.

DECLARE WITH ME

I am not behind. Heaven never said I was late. God's ways are higher than mine. My calling is not canceled. My promise is not expired. He makes everything beautiful in its time. Though it lingers, I will wait—it will certainly come. I cannot hustle my way to the promise. I release the pressure of comparison. When the time is right, the Lord will make it happen. **I am being refined—at His pace.**

JOURNAL PROMPT *(optional)*

What timeline have I created that God never set? What would it look like to open my hands and trust His timing?

DAY 16 — BOUNDARIES BEGIN WITH YOU

Think on this: Whatever is RIGHT

"Above all else, guard your heart, for everything you do flows from it." — Proverbs 4:23 (NIV)

You're running on empty—and you know exactly how you got here. Saying yes when your body screamed no. Overcommitting to avoid disappointing. Abandoning your own limits to make everyone else comfortable.

You've been giving yourself away so generously that there's almost nothing left to give.

Here's the truth no one taught you: boundaries are not walls built to keep people out. They are gates built to protect what's within.

And boundaries begin with you.

Before you can set a boundary with someone else, you have to honor the boundary within yourself. You have to believe that your limits are valid. That your capacity matters. That your "no" is just as honorable as your "yes."

Matthew 5:37 makes it plain: *Let your yes be yes and your no be no.*

No over-explaining. No guilt-laced disclaimers. No apology tours. Just truth.

But somewhere along the way, you started believing that good people don't have limits. That godly women don't say no. That love means pouring out until there's nothing left.

That's not love. That's self-abandonment.

You know when you've crossed your own limits. Your body tells you. The resentment that builds after you say yes. The exhaustion that lingers after you overcommit. The quiet anger you can't explain when you give what you didn't have to give.

These are signals—your nervous system telling you that you've been handing away what was meant to be protected.

Here's something that might shift everything: God Himself has boundaries.

He set them in creation—light from darkness, sea from land, day from night. He set them in relationship—He says yes and no with clarity and without apology. He does not adjust His nature to make everyone comfortable. He doesn't abandon who He is to manage someone else's expectations.

If the Creator has boundaries, so can you.

Boundaries are not rejection. They are stewardship. You are not responsible for managing everyone's emotions. You are responsible for stewarding what God placed in your care—your energy, your peace, your calling, your health.

Today, stop apologizing for your limits. Stop shrinking to fit into spaces that were never meant for you. Stop saying yes when your soul is screaming no.

Your boundaries are not selfish. They are sacred.

They protect the peace God is building within you.

PAUSE FOR 1 MINUTE

Draw an invisible line in front of you.

This is your boundary. It is holy.

Inhale: "My yes means yes."

Exhale: "My no means no."

Inhale: "Boundaries are not selfish."

Exhale: "Boundaries are sacred."

Even God has boundaries.

You are allowed to too.

PRAY WITH ME

Lord, I have abandoned my boundaries to keep others comfortable. I have said yes when I meant no. I have called self-abandonment love—and I'm exhausted because of it.

Forgive me.

Today, I reclaim my limits. Help me honor the capacity You've given me. Teach me to say yes and no with clarity and without guilt.

My boundaries are not walls against love—they are gates that protect it. I am not responsible for everyone else's comfort. I am responsible for stewarding what You've placed in my care.

I stop apologizing for my limits. I start protecting what's sacred.

In Jesus' name, Amen.

DECLARE WITH ME

Boundaries begin with me. My "yes" is yes. My "no" is no. I am not responsible for everyone's comfort. My limits are valid. My capacity matters. If the Creator has boundaries, so can I. Boundaries are not selfish—they are sacred.

JOURNAL PROMPT *(optional)*

Where have I abandoned my boundaries to make someone else comfortable? What is one limit I need to honor this week—starting with myself?

DAY 17 — LOOK HOW FAR YOU'VE COME

Think on this: Whatever is
PRAISEWORTHY

"I thank my God every time I remember you." — Philippians 1:3 (NIV)

Today, I want to invite you to do something you rarely give yourself permission to do: celebrate. Not the big, public kind of celebration. The quiet, sacred kind. The kind where you pause and let your soul catch up with your progress. The kind where you boast in the Lord for what He has done.

Give thanks to the Lord, for He is good. His steadfast love endures forever.

You are not where you used to be. You've grown. You've survived. You've taken steps no one else saw—and God was in every single one.

Small victories deserve a "Thank You, Jesus." Even the Apostle Paul expresses His gratitude every time He remembers God. Remembering was not nostalgia— it was worship and gratitude all in one.

The battles you've survived. The tears you've cried and wiped. The prayers you've prayed when no one else knew you were breaking. The growth that happened in secret. The healing that came slowly but surely.

You've come so far.

But the enemy wants you to forget. He wants you looking at the gap—not the gain. He wants you measuring yourself against perfection instead of remembering your progress.

Today, we pause to remember.

Philippians 1:6 says He who began a good work in you will carry it on to completion. That means you're not finished—but it also means you've already started. You're not at the beginning anymore. You're in the middle of a holy transformation.

Look at who you were a year ago. Five years ago. A decade ago.

You are not the same woman.

You've healed wounds you thought would break you. You've walked through seasons you thought would bury you. You've grown in ways you couldn't have predicted—and God was in every single step.

Don't despise your progress because it isn't perfection.

You're not where you used to be. That's worth celebrating.

Today, let your soul breathe. Let gratitude rise. Let yourself boast—not in yourself, but in what God has done. Be proud—not in arrogance, but in awe of His faithfulness.

Look how far you've come, beloved. The same God who brought you here will take you further.

PAUSE FOR 1 MINUTE

Place your hand on your heart.

Speak gently to yourself.

Inhale: "Sadness is a signal."

Exhale: "Not a sentence."

Inhale: "I can feel and still be faithful."

Exhale: "I can grieve and still have hope."

The weight you carry matters.

So does the God who carries you.

PRAY WITH ME

Lord, today I pause to celebrate. Not myself—but You. What You've done. How far You've brought me. The battles You carried me through when I didn't think I'd make it.

Give thanks to the Lord, for He is good. His steadfast love endures forever.

I remember the prayers You answered. The growth You cultivated in secret. The healing that came one day at a time. The moments I almost gave up—and didn't, because You held me.

Thank You. Thank You for not giving up on me. Thank You for every single step.

Help me celebrate without guilt. Help me boast in You without shame. Remind me that the same God who brought me here will carry me further.

You began this work. You will complete it.

In Jesus' name, Amen.

DECLARE WITH ME

I give thanks to the Lord, for He is good. His steadfast love endures forever. I am not who I used to be. I have grown in ways I couldn't have predicted. Small victories deserve celebration. He who began a good work in me will complete it. I boast in the Lord for what He has done. The same God who brought me here will carry me further. Look how far I've come.

JOURNAL PROMPT *(optional)*

What is one area of your life where you've grown significantly? What has God done that deserves a "thank You, Jesus" today? Take a moment to boast in the Lord for the progress He's made in you.

DAY 18 — THERE IS FREEDOM IN SURRENDER

Think on this: Whatever is TRUE

"Yet you, Lord, are our Father. We are the clay, you are the potter; we are all the work of your hand." — Isaiah 64:8 (NIV)

Look at your hands right now. Are they clenched? Tight? Holding something invisible but heavy?

You've been gripping so long you forgot you were doing it. Gripping outcomes. Gripping people. Gripping timelines you never had the power to control.

Your hands are tired because they've been doing God's job.

We call it strength. We call it being responsible. We call it "holding it together." But often, it's just fear dressed up as effort—control masquerading as faithfulness.

Here's what fear won't tell you: the tighter you grip, the less God can move.

Isaiah 64:8 paints the picture. We are the clay. He is the Potter. But clay that resists the Potter's hands cannot be shaped. It stays hard. It cracks under pressure. It breaks.

You've been cracking, haven't you? Breaking under the weight of what you were never meant to carry?

Surrender softens you.

Surrender isn't giving up—it's giving over. It's not weakness—it's the bravest thing you'll do today. It's the exhale that says, "God, I trust Your hands more than mine."

You've been white-knuckling what God is trying to reshape. Fighting for control when freedom was one open hand away.

So here's your invitation:

Release the outcome you've been demanding. Release the person you've been trying to fix. Release the timeline you've been gripping for dear life.

Open your hands—and watch what God does with the space.

When you stop gripping, God starts shaping. And what He shapes? It's always better than what you were clutching.

Let go. Not because you don't care—but because you finally trust the One who does.

PAUSE FOR 1 MINUTE

Look away from the comparison.

Your lane is enough.

Inhale: "I admire without comparing."

Exhale: "I celebrate without competing."

Inhale: "Her blessing is not my loss."

Exhale: "My timing is not her timing."

Stop measuring your middle

against her finish line.

PRAY WITH ME

Lord, my hands are tired.

I've been gripping plans, people, and outcomes as if everything depended on me—and I'm exhausted from carrying what was never mine to hold.

Today, I open my hands.

I release control. I release fear disguised as effort. I release the lie that says if I let go, everything falls apart.

You are the Potter. I am the clay. I stop resisting and start trusting.

Shape me. Mold me. Move in ways I could never orchestrate on my own.

I let go—not because I don't care, but because I finally believe You do.

In Jesus' name, Amen.

DECLARE WITH ME

My hands are open. Surrender is not giving up—it is giving over. I release what I was never meant to carry. I am clay in the Potter's hands. When I stop gripping, God starts shaping. What He creates is better than what I was clutching. I trust His hands more than mine.

JOURNAL PROMPT *(optional)*

What have my hands been gripping that God has been waiting for me to release? What might He shape if I finally let go?

DAY 19 — THE JOY THAT STRENGTHENS

Think on this: Whatever is LOVELY

"You make known to me the path of life; in Your presence is fullness of joy." — Psalm 16:11 (NIV)

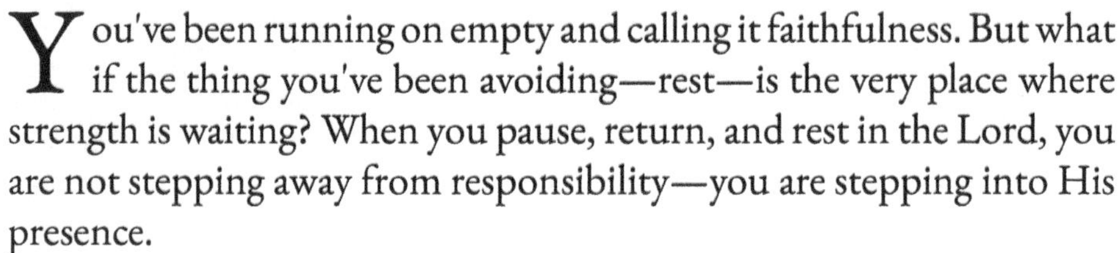

You've been running on empty and calling it faithfulness. But what if the thing you've been avoiding—rest—is the very place where strength is waiting? When you pause, return, and rest in the Lord, you are not stepping away from responsibility—you are stepping into His presence.

And Scripture is clear about what happens there.

"In Your presence is fullness of joy." — Psalm 16:11 (NIV)

Not partial joy. Not conditional joy. Fullness.

Nehemiah understood this when he spoke to a weary, overwhelmed people—people who had just rebuilt what was broken and were now undone by the weight of it all.

Picture it: dust still on their hands, walls finally standing, and instead of celebration—collapse. They wept. They were done.

And into that exhaustion, Nehemiah didn't say, "Push through." He didn't say, "Be stronger." He didn't say, "Grieve less."

He said: *"Do not grieve, for the joy of the Lord is your strength."* — Nehemiah 8:10 (NIV)

He pointed them back to joy—not as an emotion to manufacture, but as a strength that comes from the Lord.

This is why rest matters.

You've been looking for strength in all the wrong places—in productivity, in pushing through, in proving yourself. But strength was never in the grind. It was in the pause.

When you pause, you stop striving. When you return, you re-anchor your heart. When you rest, you receive.

And what you receive in His presence is joy—the kind that steadies you, fortifies you, and carries you forward.

Joy is not denial of grief. Nehemiah doesn't shame their tears—he redirects their source of strength.

Joy is not pretending you're okay. It's allowing God's presence to hold you until you are strengthened again.

Today, let yourself rest in Him. Let joy do the strengthening. You were never meant to carry this season without it.

PAUSE FOR 1 MINUTE

Let the corners of your mouth lift.

Joy is allowed here.

Inhale: "The joy of the Lord is my strength."

Exhale: "I give myself permission to smile."

Inhale: "Joy is not frivolous."

Exhale: "Joy is fuel."

Delight is not a distraction.

It's a discipline.

PRAY WITH ME

Lord, I've been running on empty and calling it faithfulness. I've looked for strength in productivity, in pushing through, in proving myself—when strength was waiting in the pause all along.

Today I stop striving and step into Your presence.

Your Word says that in Your presence there is fullness of joy, and that Your joy is my strength. I receive that now—not by effort, but by rest. Not by performance, but by trust.

Where I have been weary and undone, let Your joy steady me. Where I have been grieving, let Your presence hold me until I am strengthened again.

Teach me to rest where joy lives—in You.

In Jesus' name, Amen.

DECLARE WITH ME

I stop running on empty. I pause and return to the Lord. In His presence is fullness of joy. The joy of the Lord is my strength. Strength was never in the grind—it was in the pause. I do not grieve as one without hope. I rest. I receive. I am strengthened.

JOURNAL PROMPT *(optional)*

Where have I been looking for strength outside of God's presence? What would it feel like to let joy do the strengthening today?

DAY 20 — FORGIVE YOURSELF

Think on this: Whatever is TRUE

"As far as the east is from the west, so far has he removed our transgressions from us." — Psalm 103:12 (NIV)

You've held yourself hostage long enough for things God already released. The mistake. The failure. The thing you said. The thing you didn't say. The season you wish you could redo.

You've replayed it. You've carried shame that Jesus already carried to the cross. But here's the truth: refusing to forgive yourself is disagreeing with God's grace. God says your sins are removed—as far as the east is from the west. That's not a short distance. That's an infinite separation. He's not holding it over you. He does not keep score. He's not waiting for you to earn your way back. He's already moved it.

"If we confess our sins, he is faithful and just and will forgive us our sins and purify us from all unrighteousness." — 1 John 1:9 (NIV)

Faithful. Just. Forgiving. Purifying.

If God has done His part, why are you still doing penance?

Self-forgiveness isn't excusing what happened. It's releasing yourself from a prison God never put you in.

Today, let yourself out. Stop rehearsing the failure. Stop replaying the shame. Receive the mercy that's already been given—and extend it to yourself.

You are forgiven. Now actually forgive yourself.

PAUSE FOR 1 MINUTE

Unclench your hands.

Let go of what's holding you hostage.

Inhale: "I release them."

Exhale: "I release myself."

Inhale: "I am free."

Exhale: "Bitterness has no home here."

Forgiveness is not weakness.

It's freedom.

PRAY WITH ME

Lord, I've been holding myself hostage for things You've already forgiven. I've replayed my failures, rehearsed my shame, and refused to let myself off the hook.

But Your Word says my sins are removed—as far as the east is from the west. You're not holding them over me. Help me stop holding them over myself.

I receive Your mercy. And today, I extend that mercy to myself.

I am forgiven. I forgive myself.

In Jesus' name, Amen.

DECLARE WITH ME

God has forgiven me—I can forgive myself. My sins are removed as far as the east is from the west. I am not defined by my worst moment. I release the shame I was never meant to carry. I receive mercy—and I extend it to myself.

JOURNAL PROMPT *(optional)*

What have I been refusing to forgive myself for? What would it look like to receive God's mercy fully—and let myself off the hook?

DAY 21 — SADNESS DOESN'T GET TO CRUSH YOU

Think on this: Whatever is TRUE

"The Lord is close to the brokenhearted and saves those who are crushed in spirit." — Psalm 34:18 (NIV)

Sadness has been sitting on your chest, and you've been pretending it's not there. Maybe it came with a name—grief, disappointment, loss. Maybe it arrived without explanation—a heaviness you can't trace, a sorrow that lingers without reason.

Sometimes sadness doesn't announce itself. Sometimes it's your body remembering what your mind is too exhausted to process. Sometimes it's the weariness in your soul because boundaries are absent. Seasons that shifted, or dreams that didn't unfold the way you hoped.

You don't have to understand your sadness to be gentle with yourself in it.

But here's what you need to know: sadness is a signal, not a sentence. It's telling you something needs attention—but it doesn't get to define your future.

Psalm 34:18 says the Lord is *close* to the brokenhearted. Not distant. Not disappointed. Close.

He doesn't scold you for struggling. He draws near.

Sadness is allowed to visit—but it doesn't get to set up shop. It doesn't get to crush you. It doesn't get to have the final word.

Sometimes your nervous system holds memories your thoughts have moved past. Be patient with your body. Be kind to your heart.

Today, let yourself feel what's there—but don't let it own you. God is near. And near is where healing begins.

PAUSE FOR 1 MINUTE

Let the tears come if they need to.

Sadness is allowed to visit.

Inhale: "God is close to the brokenhearted."

Exhale: "He saves those crushed in spirit."

Inhale: "I don't have to be strong right now."

Exhale: "I can be held."

Sadness is a visitor.

Not a resident.

PRAY WITH ME

Lord, I've been carrying sadness I didn't know how to name. Some of it makes sense. Some of it doesn't.

But I know You are close—closer than the ache, closer than the tears.

I don't have to perform my way out of this. I just have to let You near.

Hold me in the heaviness. Heal what's broken. And remind me that sadness doesn't get to stay forever.

In Jesus' name, Amen.

DECLARE WITH ME

Sadness is allowed to visit—it doesn't get to stay. The Lord is close to the brokenhearted. I don't have to understand my sadness to be gentle with myself. Sadness is a signal, not a sentence. I am held while I heal.

JOURNAL PROMPT *(optional)*

What sadness have I been carrying that I haven't acknowledged? What would it mean to let God draw near to it today?

DAY 22 — DON'T LET THE COMPARISON THIEF IN

Think on this: Whatever is
ADMIRABLE

"For we are God's handiwork, created in Christ Jesus to do good works, which God prepared in advance for us to do." — Ephesians 2:10 (NIV)

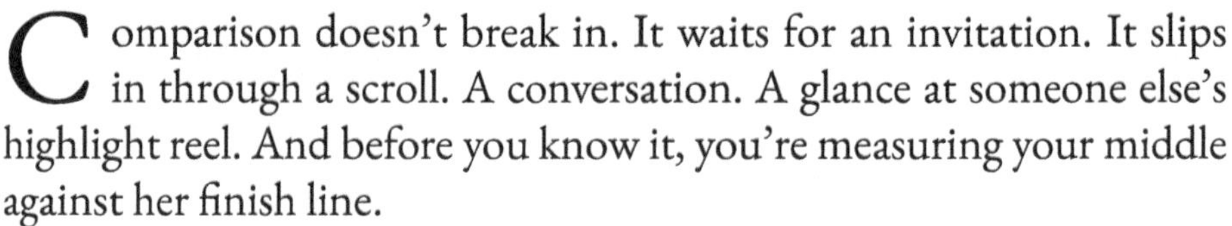

Comparison doesn't break in. It waits for an invitation. It slips in through a scroll. A conversation. A glance at someone else's highlight reel. And before you know it, you're measuring your middle against her finish line.

But you were never meant to compare. You were created to admire.

There's a difference.

Admiration says, *"Look what God is doing."* Comparison says, *"Why isn't He doing that for me?"*

One leads to worship. The other leads to a wound.

Ephesians 2:10 says you are God's handiwork—His masterpiece. Created in Christ Jesus for good works that He prepared in advance for *you* to do. Not her works. Not their calling. Yours.

When you compare, you dismiss the unique design God placed in you. You devalue the path He's crafting specifically for your feet.

She is your sister, not your standard. Her success doesn't diminish yours. Her blessing doesn't limit what God has for you.

When one woman wins, we all do.

Today, close the door on comparison. Admire without envy. Celebrate without competing. And remember—your lane is the only one that matters.

PAUSE FOR 1 MINUTE

Stand firm. Plant your feet.

Fear is a liar.

Inhale: "I am not given a spirit of fear."

Exhale: "But of power, love, and a sound mind."

Inhale: "Fear does not lead me."

Exhale: "God does."

Courage isn't the absence of fear.

It's moving forward anyway.

PRAY WITH ME

Lord, I've let comparison steal my peace. I've measured my journey against someone else's and come up feeling behind.

But You made me on purpose, for a purpose. My design is intentional. My calling is specific. My lane is mine.

Help me admire without envy. Celebrate without competing. And remember that when one woman wins, we all do.

In Jesus' name, Amen.

DECLARE WITH ME

I was created to admire, not compare. She is my sister, not my standard. Her success doesn't threaten mine. I am God's handiwork—uniquely designed. I stay in my lane and trust my timing.

JOURNAL PROMPT *(optional)*

Who have I been comparing myself to? What would it look like to admire her journey without devaluing my own?

DAY 23 — GOD HEARS THE CRY YOU DON'T SAY OUT LOUD

Think on this: Whatever is TRUE

"Before they call I will answer; while they are still speaking I will hear."
— Isaiah 65:24 (NIV)

Some prayers are too heavy for words. You've had moments where all you could do was breathe—because the ache was too deep to articulate.

Where the tears fell but the sentences didn't form.

Where you wanted to pray but didn't know what to say.

And you wondered if God heard you anyway.

He did.

Isaiah 65:24 says, *"Before they call I will answer; while they are still speaking I will hear."*

Before you form the sentence, He's already leaning in. Before you find the words, He's already responding.

And Romans 8:26 reminds us that when we don't know how to pray, the Spirit intercedes for us with groans too deep for words.

You don't have to get the prayer right. You don't have to be eloquent. You don't have to perform for God to pay attention.

Silence is still prayer. A breath is still reaching. A tear is still heard.

Today, release the pressure to pray perfectly. Let your soul groan. Let your spirit sigh. God is not waiting for polished words—He's listening for your heart.

And your heart? He's already heard it.

PAUSE FOR 1 MINUTE

You don't need words.

A breath is still a prayer.

Inhale: "Before I call, He answers."

Exhale: "He hears what I cannot say."

Inhale: "My sighs are heard."

Exhale: "My tears are seen."

God hears the cry you don't say out loud.

He understands.

PRAY WITH ME

Lord, sometimes I don't have the words. Sometimes the ache is too deep to articulate and the prayer gets stuck in my chest.

But You hear me anyway. Before I call, You answer. While I'm still speaking, You're already listening.

Thank You for not needing polished prayers. Thank You for hearing the cry I don't say out loud.

I trust that You know what I need—even when I can't say it.

In Jesus' name, Amen.

DECLARE WITH ME

God hears the cry I don't say out loud. Before I call, He answers. My silence is still prayer. I don't have to perform to be heard. He knows what I need before I ask.

JOURNAL PROMPT *(optional)*

What prayer have I been afraid to speak—or unable to articulate? What would it mean to trust that God already heard it?

DAY 24 — REPLAY TESTIMONY, NOT TORMENT

Think on this: Whatever is
EXCELLENT

"They triumphed over him by the blood of the Lamb and by the word of their testimony." — Revelation 12:11 (NIV)

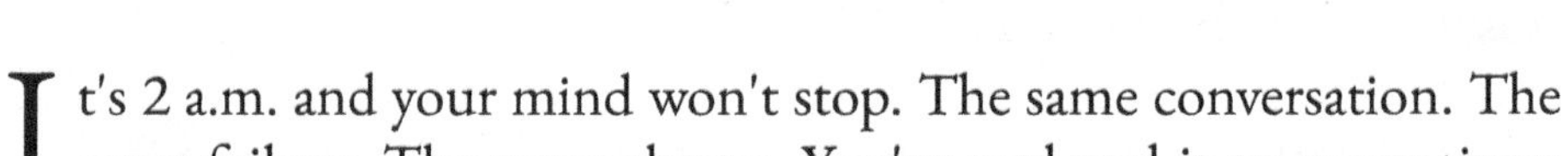

It's 2 a.m. and your mind won't stop. The same conversation. The same failure. The same shame. You've replayed it so many times you've memorized the pain.

Your mind is always replaying something. The question is: what track is on repeat?

For too long, you've been replaying the torment. The rejection. The thing someone said that you can't unhear. The moment you fell apart and wondered if you'd ever get back up.

You've replayed it so many times your body tenses just thinking about it. Your chest tightens. Your stomach drops. The shame washes over you like it just happened yesterday.

That's torment on loop. And it's been draining you.

But Revelation 12:11 says we overcome by the blood of the Lamb and the word of our testimony.

Your testimony isn't just a story—it's a weapon. It smashes the life out of shame.

When you rehearse what God has done, you remind the enemy—and yourself—that God is faithful. That He's come through before. That He'll come through again.

The Psalmist understood this: *"Come and hear, all you who fear God; let me tell you what he has done for me."* — Psalm 66:16 (NIV)

Here's the shift: stop replaying what was done to you and start replaying what God did for you.

Your testimony is louder than your trauma. Your praise is more powerful than your pain.

Today, change the track. When the torment starts to replay—when your mind drifts back to the rejection, the failure, the shame—hit pause. And press play on testimony instead.

Remember the time He provided when you thought you'd go without. Remember the door He opened when every other one closed. Remember the peace He gave when everything around you was falling apart.

That's your weapon. Use it.

PAUSE FOR 1 MINUTE

Shift your focus.

Replay the testimony, not the torment.

Inhale: "I replay testimony."

Exhale: "Not torment."

Inhale: "God has been faithful before."

Exhale: "He will be faithful again."

Your testimony is louder than your trauma.

Tell it.

PRAY WITH ME

Lord, I've been replaying the wrong things. The pain. The failure. The moments I wish I could forget. The torment has been on loop—and I'm exhausted from it.

Today, I change the track.

I choose to remember what You've done—the ways You've come through, the prayers You've answered, the battles You've won on my behalf.

My testimony is louder than my trauma. Help me wield it as the weapon it was meant to be.

In Jesus' name, Amen.

DECLARE WITH ME

I replay testimony, not torment. My testimony is a weapon—I wield it with faith. What God did for me is louder than what was done to me. I overcome by the blood of the Lamb and the word of my testimony. I change the track—and press play on praise.

JOURNAL PROMPT *(optional)*

What testimony have I forgotten to celebrate? What has God done for me that deserves to be on repeat instead of the pain?

DAY 25 — LET GRACE ABOUND

Think on this: Whatever is TRUE

"But where sin increased, grace increased all the more."
— Romans 5:20 (NIV)

You've been striving for grace you already have. Your shoulders are tight from carrying the weight of being enough. Your mind is exhausted from keeping score. And somewhere along the way, you started believing that grace was something you had to earn.

Trying to be good enough. Trying to prove you deserve it. Trying to balance the scales between your failures and your faithfulness.

But grace doesn't work that way.

Romans 5:20 says where sin increased, grace increased *all the more*. Not just enough to cover you—more than enough. Abounding. Overflowing. Excessive.

And here's what trips us up: Isaiah 64:6 says all our righteous acts are like filthy rags. Not our sins—our righteousness. Even our best efforts can't earn what only grace can give.

You sin daily. So does everyone. So did Paul. So did David. So did Peter. That's not an excuse—it's the reason grace exists.

If righteousness could be earned, grace wouldn't be necessary. But you can't out-perform your need for mercy.

"My grace is sufficient for you, for my power is made perfect in weakness." — 2 Corinthians 12:9 (NIV)

Grace isn't the backup plan. It's the only plan.

Today, stop striving. Start receiving. Let grace abound in your weakness, your failure, your not-enough-ness.

You don't need to earn it. You just need to let it in.

PAUSE FOR 1 MINUTE

Open your hands to receive.

Grace is not earned. It is given.

Inhale: "Grace is not earned."

Exhale: "Grace is received."

Inhale: "I stop striving."

Exhale: "I start receiving."

You can't out-perform your need for mercy.

Rest in grace.

PRAY WITH ME

Lord, I've been trying to earn what You already gave. I've been striving to prove I'm worthy of grace—when the whole point is that I'm not.

Today, I stop performing. I stop trying to balance the scales. I receive what I could never deserve.

Your grace is sufficient. Your power is perfect in my weakness. I let grace abound.

In Jesus' name, Amen.

DECLARE WITH ME

Grace is not earned—grace is received. Where sin increases, grace increases more. I cannot out-perform my need for mercy. His grace is sufficient for me. I stop striving and start receiving.

JOURNAL PROMPT *(optional)*

Where have I been striving to earn grace instead of receiving it? What would it feel like to stop performing and just let grace be enough?

DAY 26 — YOU ARE A HUMAN BEING, NOT A HUMAN DOING

Think on this: Whatever is TRUE

"Be still, and know that I am God." — Psalm 46:10 (NIV)

You've been measuring your value by your productivity. Busy has become your badge of honor. Your to-do list has become your report card. And somewhere along the way, you forgot that you're a human being—not a human doing. But God didn't design you to earn your worth through work. He established your value before you accomplished anything.

Psalm 46:10 says, *"Be still, and know that I am God."*

Not "be productive." Not "be impressive." Be still.

Stillness is not laziness. Rest is not weakness. Pausing is not falling behind.

Jesus invites the weary—not the productive—to come and receive rest:

"Come to me, all you who are weary and burdened, and I will give you rest." — Matthew 11:28 (NIV)

He doesn't ask for your résumé. He asks for your presence.

The most productive thing you can do today might be to stop producing altogether. To sit. To breathe. To remember that you are loved not for what you do—but for who you are.

Your worth was established before you did a single thing. It doesn't increase with accomplishment or decrease with failure.

Today, let yourself *be*. You are a human being. Start there.

PAUSE FOR 1 MINUTE

Stop doing. Just be.

You are a human being, not a human doing.

Inhale: "I am."

Exhale: "That is enough."

Inhale: "I don't have to produce to have value."

Exhale: "I am valuable because I exist."

Your worth is not in your output.

It's in your identity.

PRAY WITH ME

Lord, I've been measuring my worth by my productivity. I've believed the lie that my value is tied to my output.

But You call me to be still. You invite the weary, not the impressive.

Today, I release the pressure to perform. I rest in who I am—not what I do. I am Yours, and that is enough.

In Jesus' name, Amen.

DECLARE WITH ME

I am a human being, not a human doing. My worth is not tied to my output. Stillness is not laziness. Rest is not weakness. I am loved for who I am, not what I produce. I release the pressure to perform.

JOURNAL PROMPT *(optional)*

How much of my identity has been tied to productivity? What would it feel like to rest in who I am instead of what I do?

DAY 27 — DON'T HIDE FROM LOVE

Think on this: Whatever is LOVELY

"There is no fear in love. But perfect love drives out fear."
— 1 John 4:18 (NIV)

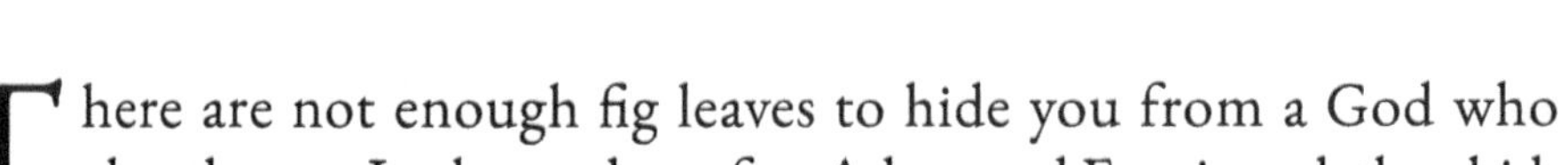

There are not enough fig leaves to hide you from a God who already sees. In the garden, after Adam and Eve sinned, they hid. And God called out, *"Where are you?"*

Not because He didn't know—but because He wanted them to come out of hiding.

He's asking you the same thing today.

Where are you?

Not geographically—but relationally. Have you been hiding from His love because you feel unworthy? Have you been keeping distance because you're ashamed?

But perfect love doesn't wait for you to clean up. It doesn't demand perfection before it pursues. It comes looking for you—even in the bushes, even in the mess, even in the shame.

"See, I have engraved you on the palms of my hands." — Isaiah 49:16 (NIV)

You are inscribed on His hands. You cannot escape His presence—and His presence is love.

"Where can I go from your Spirit? Where can I flee from your presence?" — Psalm 139:7 (NIV)

You cannot outrun Him. You cannot hide from Him. And here's the good news: you don't have to.

You cannot break His heart by being honest about yours. He already knows—and He's not leaving.

God is love. And His love is holding you even now.

PAUSE FOR 1 MINUTE

Remove the mask. Just for this moment.

You are safe to be seen.

Inhale: "I am safe to be seen."

Exhale: "I am safe to be known."

Inhale: "Authenticity is freedom."

Exhale: "Hiding is exhausting."

You don't have to pretend here.

God sees all of you and loves all of you.

PRAY WITH ME

Lord, I've been hiding. From Your love. From Your presence. From the vulnerability of being fully known.

But You called out to Adam—not because You didn't know where he was, but because You wanted him to come out.

Today, I come out. I stop hiding. I let Your perfect love drive out my fear.

I am Yours. And I receive Your love—fully.

In Jesus' name, Amen.

DECLARE WITH ME

I stop hiding from Love. Perfect love drives out fear. I am engraved on the palms of His hands. I cannot break God's heart by being honest about mine. I let myself be found.

JOURNAL PROMPT *(optional)*

What have I been hiding from God? What would it look like to come out of hiding and let His love find me?

DAY 28 — YOU ARE NOT THE SUM OF YOUR STRUGGLES

Think on this: Whatever is TRUE

"Fear not, for I have redeemed you; I have summoned you by name; you are mine." — Isaiah 43:1 (NIV)

You've been introducing yourself by what you've been through instead of who God says you are. *"I'm the anxious one." "I'm the broken one." "I'm the one with the disorder." "I'm the one who can't seem to get it together."*

But that's not your name. That's not your identity.

Here's what happens when we speak something: we hear it twice—once in our mind, once out loud. And when we hear it, our brain creates a neural pathway. We train ourselves to identify with the wound instead of the Word.

"Can two walk together unless they agree?" — Amos 3:3 (NKJV)

Every time you agree with trauma, you walk with the wrong voice. Every time you name yourself by your pain, you partner with the lie.

But Psalm 23 shows us another way. The Lord leads us *through* the valley—we don't set up residence there. We don't unpack our bags. We don't accessorize our identity with affliction.

Notice the order: *"He leads me in paths of righteousness"* comes before the valley. The valley is not your destination—it's a passage. And God walks with you through it.

Today, I want to offer you a reframe:

You are not anxious—you are anchored. You are not broken—you are being restored. You are not disordered—you are being renewed. You are not depressed—you are learning to hope again.

"Therefore, if anyone is in Christ, the new creation has come: The old has gone, the new is here!" — 2 Corinthians 5:17 (NIV)

You were never becoming someone else. You were returning to who God already said you are. That identity was never lost—just covered.

Healing begins when you stop rehearsing pain as identity and start submitting your mind to truth.

PAUSE FOR 1 MINUTE

Speak this over yourself:

You are not your worst moment.

Inhale: "I am not what I have done."

Exhale: "I am who He says I am."

Inhale: "Shame has no hold on me."

Exhale: "I am free."

Your past does not define you.

His Word does.

PRAY WITH ME

Lord, I've been calling myself by my struggles. I've let my wounds become my name.

But You call me by a different name. You say I am redeemed. Chosen. Yours.

Today, I stop agreeing with the wrong voice. I stop identifying with my pain. I submit my mind to Your truth.

I am not the sum of my struggles. I am Yours.

In Jesus' name, Amen.

DECLARE WITH ME

I am not the sum of my struggles. I am not what I've been through—I am who God says I am. I walk through the valley—I don't live there. My identity is not my affliction. I am redeemed, summoned by name, and I am His.

JOURNAL PROMPT *(optional)*

How have I been identifying myself by my struggles? What name does God call me instead?

DAY 29 — PEACE IS NOT A PLACE—HE IS A PERSON

Think on this: Whatever is GOOD
REPORT

"For he himself is our peace." — Ephesians 2:14 (NIV)

You've been chasing peace like it's a destination. "I'll have peace when the bills are paid." "I'll have peace when the kids are settled." "I'll have peace when this season is over."

But peace was never a place you arrive at. Peace is a Person you return to. Ephesians 2:14 says, "He himself is our peace." Not He gives peace—He *is* peace.

And in John 14:27, Jesus said, "Peace I leave with you; my peace I give you. I do not give to you as the world gives."

The world offers peace that depends on circumstance—peace that comes and goes with the bills, the diagnosis, the relationship status. But Jesus offers peace that transcends circumstance. Peace that holds steady when nothing else does.

He passed His own peace to you—the same peace He carried to the cross, through the tomb, and out the other side. Not temporary calm. Transcendent peace.

Isaiah 26:3 says, "You will keep in perfect peace those whose minds are steadfast, because they trust in you."

Perfect peace—spirit, soul, and body aligned—comes from keeping your mind fixed on Him. Not on the problem. Not on the timeline. On Him.

You don't have to chase what's already holding you.

PAUSE FOR 1 MINUTE

Stop searching. Peace is not a place.

Peace is a Person.

Inhale: "Peace is not a place."

Exhale: "Peace is a Person."

Inhale: "Jesus is my peace."

Exhale: "I carry Him with me."

You don't have to chase what's already holding you.

Rest.

PRAY WITH ME

Lord, I've been chasing peace like it was somewhere out there—beyond the next accomplishment, the next breakthrough, the next resolution.

But You are my peace. Not a feeling I find—but a Person I return to.

Today, I stop running. I stop striving. I rest in You—the Prince of Peace, the One who holds all things together, including me.

I don't have to chase what's already holding me.

In Jesus' name, Amen.

DECLARE WITH ME

Jesus doesn't just give peace—He is peace. Peace is not a place—it's a Person. I stop chasing and start returning. My mind is fixed on Him, and He keeps me in perfect peace. I don't have to chase what's already holding me.

JOURNAL PROMPT *(optional)*

Where have I been looking for peace outside of Jesus? What would change if I stopped chasing and started returning?

DAY 30 — BE LED BY TRUTH, NOT EMOTIONS

PRACTICE THESE THINGS

"Whatever you have learned or received or heard from me, or seen in me—put it into practice. And the God of peace will be with you."
— Philippians 4:9 (NIV)

Emotions are real—but they're not always reliable. They're indicators, not drivers. Lights on the dashboard, not hands on the wheel. For too long, you've let feelings dictate your direction. Fear said run—so you ran. Anxiety said spiral—so you spiraled. Sadness said stay down—so you stayed.

But today, we shift the order.

Feel what you feel—then ask, "What is actually true?"

The truth is: you are held. You are seen. You are not behind. You are not forgotten. You are not defined by your worst moment or your hardest season.

And you've been practicing this. Thirty days of pausing. Thirty days of returning. Thirty days of choosing truth over chaos.

You didn't wait until you were empty to return. You learned to return to stay full.

Your pause is proactive now—not reactive. You reset by design, not by default. You've moved from surviving to stewarding your peace.

This is what transformation looks like. Not perfection—but rhythm. Not arrival—but return.

You were never becoming someone else. You were returning to who God already said you are. That identity was never lost—just buried under exhaustion, fear, and the noise of a world that never stops demanding.

Over these thirty days, you've been uncovering it.

And now? You practice these things. Not perfectly. Not without stumbling. But intentionally. Daily. By design.

The God of peace will be with you.

PAUSE FOR 1 MINUTE

Place your hand on your heart one last time.

You made it. Thirty days of returning.

Inhale: "I am led by truth."

Exhale: "Not driven by emotion."

Inhale: "I practice these things."

Exhale: "The God of peace is with me."

This is not the end.

This is the rhythm you return to.

PRAY WITH ME

Lord, I've let emotions lead me for too long. Fear. Anxiety. Sadness. They've had the wheel—and I've been exhausted.

But today, I take it back. I choose to be led by truth. I let my emotions inform me—but I don't let them drive.

Thank You for these thirty days. Thank You for meeting me in every pause, every breath, every return.

I am not who I was. I am who You say I am. And I will keep practicing these things—not perfectly, but faithfully.

The God of peace is with me.

In Jesus' name, Amen.

DECLARE WITH ME

I am led by truth, not driven by emotion. My pause is proactive—not reactive. I reset by design, not by default. I don't wait until I'm empty to return—I return to stay full. I practice these things. The God of peace is with me. I am who God says I am—and I keep returning to Him.

JOURNAL PROMPT *(optional)*

What has shifted in me over these thirty days? How has my pause moved from reactive to proactive? What will I continue to practice?

GO WITH PEACE

And the God of peace will be with you." — Philippians 4:9 (NIV)

You've spent thirty days doing both—pursuing peace and practicing it.

Returning to what is true, noble, right, pure, lovely, admirable, excellent, and praiseworthy.

These weren't just concepts—they were rhythms.

You don't need an hour.

Five minutes—that's it.

Now go. Pause. Return. And let peace lead. You showed up for thirty days. Not perfectly — but faithfully. And that's what this was always about. Not performance. Not mastery. Just returning. Again and again, back to the truth, back to the pause, back to the God who was never in a hurry with you.

This isn't the end of the rhythm. It's the beginning of it.

"Think on these things... practice these things... and the God of peace will be with you." — Philippians 4:8–9

ABOUT THE AUTHOR

Merline Ulloth is a writer, speaker, and faith-based coach passionate about creating authentic spaces for Christian women to heal and walk in the fullness of their God-given identity and freedom in Jesus.

An Army veteran, Merline knows what it means to carry weight that was never meant to be carried alone. In 2020, a life-altering accident brought her face-to-face with the necessity of rest, renewal, and trusting God in the pause. Out of that season, **the Uncommon U** was born—with a mission to equip high-functioning women to be transformed by the renewing of their minds, rest in God's presence, and rise in purpose—whole, healthy, and complete.

Pause for 5 on 5: Transformational Mindset Renewal is her debut book and an invitation to do just that.

When she's not writing or coaching, Merline enjoys quiet mornings with Jesus, nature walks, exploring coffee shops, serving in her local church, and spending time with her children and family.

Connect with Merline:

www.theuncommonu.com

@theuncommonu on Instagram and Facebook

Thank you for pausing with me.

— Merline

www.ingramcontent.com/pod-product-compliance
Lightning Source LLC
Chambersburg PA
CBHW030900120726
48008CB00002B/59